MVFOL

Science Matters! | Volume 21

Dissolving

A brief history

TODAY... 1823 Charles Macintosh, a Scottish scientist, dissolves rubber in a liquid called naptha and uses it to waterproof fabric... 1819 John Kidd, an English chemist, separates coal tar from an oil-like liquid, paving the way for the discovery of other substances dissolved in oil, such as gasoline... 1808 Joseph Louis Proust extracts sugars from plant juices, showing that food substances are dissolved in plant juices... 1803 William Henry, a British chemist, finds that a larger amount of gas can be dissolved in a liquid if the liquid is put under pressure... 1801 John Dalton, a British chemist, proposes the theory of atoms, which states that all materials are made of small particles called atoms. Since atoms are the smallest particles, the atoms of a dissolved substance must be scattered evenly among the atoms of the liquid it is dissolved in... 1777 Carl Wenzel, a German chemist, finds that the amount of a substance that will dissolve varies with the substance used and the liquid it is dissolved in... 1756 Scottish scientist Joseph Black experiments with solutions, giving the first detailed account of how substances combine... About 340 B.C. Aristotle, Greek philosopher, describes the way that liquids can dissolve other liquids, gases, and solids... For thousands of years people boiled plants in water to make natural dyes used to color their cloth.

Dr. Brian Knapp

Word list

These are some science words that you should look out for as you go through the book. They are shown using CAPITAL letters.

BOIL/BOILING
Heating a liquid until it has so much energy that it turns into a gas.

CONCENTRATED
A liquid that contains a relatively large amount of dissolved substance.

CONDENSATION
Turning from a gas into a liquid.

CRYSTAL
A solid that has a regular shape, with flat sides meeting at sharp angles.

DISSOLVE
To break up into tiny particles within a liquid.

ENERGY
The ability to make something happen. Heat energy makes a liquid boil and turn into a gas.

EVAPORATE
To turn from a liquid into a gas.

FILTER
To separate a solid from a liquid by pouring the mixture through a substance with very small holes (also called a filter).

GAS
A form of a substance in which the particles are not touching and are free to move around. A gas spreads out to fill as much space as it can.

HARD WATER
Water that has a lot of natural substances dissolved in it.

INSOLUBLE
A substance that will not dissolve at all in a particular liquid.

LIQUID
A form of a substance in which the particles are free to move around, but they still remain close to each other.

MIXTURE
A combination of two or more substances that have become stirred together.

PARTICLES
Pieces of a substance that are too small to be seen except with special microscopes.

POLLUTION
Adding unnatural substances to the environment. For example, water may be polluted by factories, farms, and homes if care is not taken to clean water after we use it.

POROUS
A substance that has small connecting holes in it.

SEPARATE
To take one substance from another.

SOLID
A form of a substance in which the particles are attached together. A solid keeps a fixed shape unless it is pushed, squeezed, or pulled.

SOLUBLE
A substance that will dissolve easily in a particular liquid.

SOLUTION
A mixture of a liquid with another liquid, a solid, or a gas.

SUBSTANCE
Something that is pure and not a mixture.

SUSPENSION
A mixture of small particles in a liquid. The particles are not dissolved in the liquid, and in time they will settle out.

Contents

What is dissolving?

When something DISSOLVES, it breaks up into tiny pieces that scatter evenly in a LIQUID.

Have you ever stirred a spoonful of sugar into a cup of hot water and wondered where the sugar went? The sugar seems to just disappear, but we know that it hasn't vanished because the water tastes sugary. So what has happened to the sugar?

It is similar to when you put a spoonful of instant coffee in a cup of clear, hot water—the coffee dissolves, and the water turns brown (Picture 1).

The brown color is a clue as to what has happened. The coffee powder, or granules, were brown, and now the water is brown. Large pieces of coffee have been pulled apart into tiny pieces and then scattered evenly within the water. This is what happened to the sugar, too.

The sugar and coffee are still in the water, but now they are all mixed together with the water. In the case of the coffee the brown color shows you so. If you tasted the water, you would be able to taste both the coffee and the sugar. The coffee, the sugar, and the water are still separate from one another; the sugar and the coffee only *seem* to

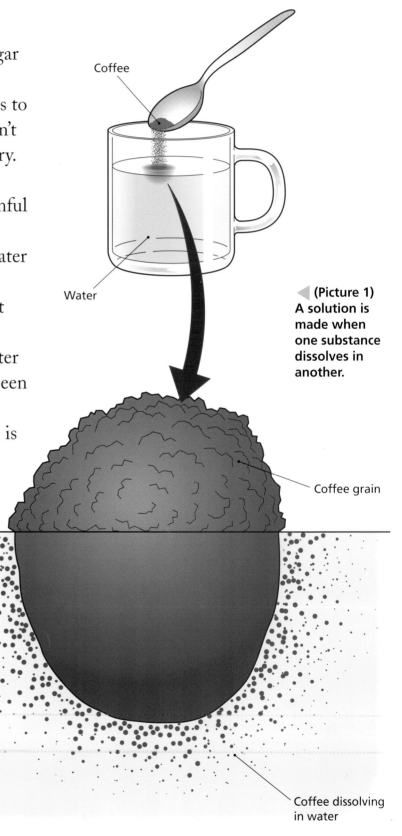

Coffee

Water

◀ **(Picture 1) A solution is made when one substance dissolves in another.**

Coffee grain

Coffee dissolving in water

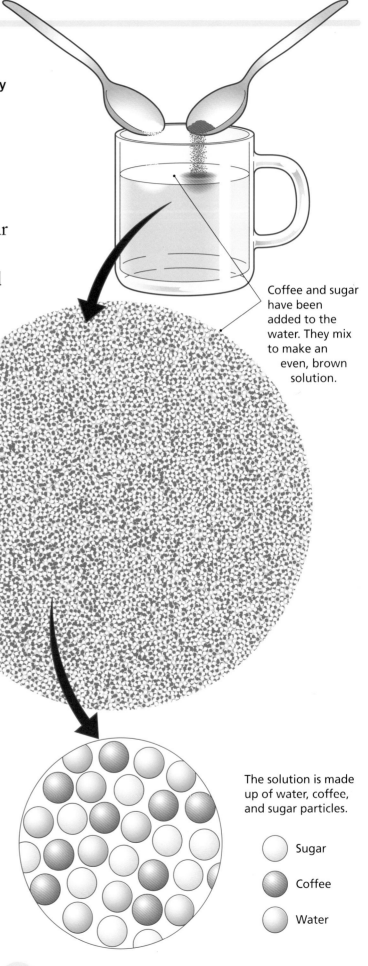

▶ **(Picture 2)** In a solution the PARTICLES of one substance are evenly scattered through the other.

have become part of the water (Picture 2). The coffee and the sugar have dissolved in the water.

When a **SUBSTANCE** seems to disappear into a liquid, we say it has dissolved. The **MIXTURE** it forms with the liquid is called a **SOLUTION**. The substance has become part of the liquid.

What will dissolve?

SOLIDS, liquids, and **GASES** all dissolve in liquids. When you put coffee powder into water, you are dissolving a solid into a liquid. When you put a few drops of food coloring into water, you are dissolving one liquid in another. The only reason that fish can breathe in water is that air (which is an invisible gas) is dissolved in the water.

 SAFETY Never go near boiling water. Always get an adult to help.

Coffee and sugar have been added to the water. They mix to make an even, brown solution.

The solution is made up of water, coffee, and sugar particles.

◯ Sugar

◯ Coffee

◯ Water

Summary

- When a substance dissolves in a liquid, it breaks up into tiny particles that scatter evenly in the liquid.
- A solution is a mixture of two or more substances.
- When a substance dissolves in water, it forms a solution.

What is in dirty water?

Dirty water is a mixture of very tiny PARTICLES—some of which have dissolved and others that have not.

Water is very good at carrying other substances. Some substances dissolve in the same way as coffee grains and are carried in solution. Other substances are carried along only when water is flowing swiftly. The mud carried by rivers during a flood is like this. The mud does not dissolve but instead is suspended in the water. We say the mud is in **SUSPENSION**. This happens quite naturally and in a way that is not harmful. However, when people or factories are careless with their waste, it can also dissolve in water and cause **POLLUTION** (Picture 1). To prevent this, we treat the water in a water-treatment plant.

Cleaning up dirty water means that both suspended and dissolved substances must be removed from water.

Settling out

Given enough time, suspended substances will settle out of water. Settling is slow and may take many weeks (Picture 2).

Filtering

If a substance is only suspended in a liquid, it has not become part of the

▲ (Picture 1) Very dirty water flowing in a river in a city. This water has scum on the surface, and the water itself is a dark gray due to pollution.

▶ (Picture 2) A water-treatment plant uses big ponds to allow suspended substances to settle out, then the water is filtered through large circular beds of sand. Only then are the dissolved substances treated.

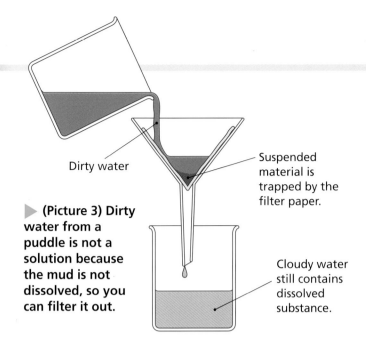

Dirty water

Suspended material is trapped by the filter paper.

▶ (Picture 3) Dirty water from a puddle is not a solution because the mud is not dissolved, so you can filter it out.

Cloudy water still contains dissolved substance.

▼ (Picture 4) Substances in solution are so small they cannot be separated from the water by pouring them through a filter paper. Substances that are completely dissolved, like ink, can be poured straight through a filter paper without being trapped.

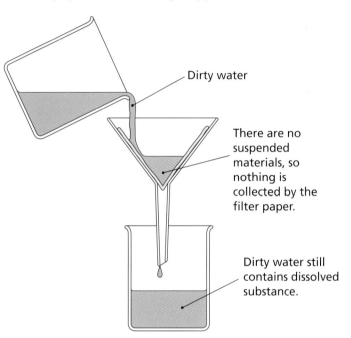

Dirty water

There are no suspended materials, so nothing is collected by the filter paper.

Dirty water still contains dissolved substance.

liquid. As a result, we can **FILTER** it out. Pouring muddy water through a filter paper, for example, will remove all of the material suspended in the water but not the dissolved material (Picture 3). In this way the filter paper **SEPARATES** out the suspended substance from the dissolved substance. If you pour all of the water through the filter paper and nothing is left behind on the filter paper, then everything has dissolved in the water (Picture 4).

What remains

You will find that after filtering a muddy pool or wash water, the water will probably still be cloudy. That is because some substances are dissolved in it.

Even if it is clear, it can still contain dissolved substances, because not all dissolved substances are colored (as we saw on page 4 with dissolving sugar).

The next step is to remove the dissolved substances. A way of doing that is shown on page 20.

Summary
- Dirty water can carry unwanted substances.
- Some substances can be removed by filtering and settling.
- Water can look clean and still be polluted.

How much will dissolve?

There is a limit to how much of a substance will dissolve in a liquid. It varies between substances and also depends on how hot they are.

When you make a cup of instant coffee, you put coffee, and perhaps sugar, into hot water. Soon these ingredients have dissolved, or blended together, and made a cup of steaming hot coffee. But if someone had a sweet tooth or wanted very strong coffee, could they keep putting sugar and coffee into the cup forever?

Are all substances equally soluble?

Substances vary widely in how much they will dissolve. If a substance will not dissolve, it is called **INSOLUBLE** (Picture 1). If it will dissolve, it is **SOLUBLE**.

There is no easy way to guess whether something is soluble or insoluble. You simply have to try it to find out.

Comparing substances

It is easy to find out how much of a substance will dissolve in water. You need a glass or clear, plastic-sided jar so that you can see what is happening. Use the same amount of water for each test. You simply add whatever substance you are testing (for example, sugar, bath salts, or table salt) to the water one spoonful at a time. After each new spoonful is added, you have to stir until everything dissolves (Picture 2). That may take a few minutes, especially when the solution contains almost as much of the substance as it will take.

Finally, a stage will be reached when you add a spoonful, but it will not dissolve, and some solid remains in the bottom. That is the point when you have

▼ **(Picture 1) Many substances will not dissolve in water. Vegetable oil is one liquid that will not dissolve in water. Sand is a solid that will not dissolve in water.**

The vegetable oil floats on water, it does not dissolve.

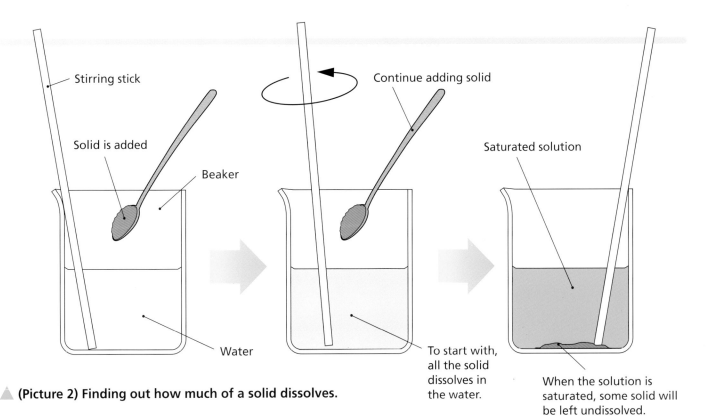

Stirring stick

Solid is added

Beaker

Water

Continue adding solid

To start with, all the solid dissolves in the water.

Saturated solution

When the solution is saturated, some solid will be left undissolved.

▲ **(Picture 2) Finding out how much of a solid dissolves.**

added as much of the substance as will dissolve in that amount of water. We say the solution is saturated.

If you find out, for example, that you can dissolve more spoonfuls of bath salts than spoonfuls of sugar, then we say that the bath salts are more soluble than the sugar.

You can compare all kinds of substances in the same way (Picture 3), but it is important to always use water at the same temperature; for example, always use water at room temperature. You will find out why this is so important on the next page.

Summary
- **Not all substances dissolve in water.**
- **Different substances dissolve in water by different amounts.**
- **There is a limit to how much of a substance can be dissolved.**

▼ **(Picture 3) It may seem surprising, but the same amount of water will dissolve different amounts of chemical. The ones below are from a chemist's laboratory. Each chemical will dissolve in 100ml of water at room temperature. As you can see, some substances are far more soluble than others.**

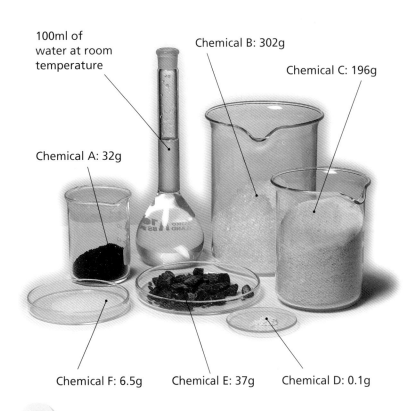

100ml of water at room temperature

Chemical B: 302g

Chemical C: 196g

Chemical A: 32g

Chemical F: 6.5g

Chemical E: 37g

Chemical D: 0.1g

Speeding up dissolving

A solid dissolves faster when it is made into a powder, if it is stirred into the liquid, or when the liquid is warmer.

It is often quite important to get substances to dissolve quickly. For example, when you make a cup of instant coffee, you want the coffee to dissolve very quickly so that the water doesn't get cold before you drink it.

Dissolving can be speeded up in several ways. The normal ways are:

1. To crush the solid into a powder.
2. To stir the solid with the water.
3. To warm the water and the solid.

Lump or powder?

A lump of substance will dissolve much more slowly than when the same substance is made into a powder (Picture 1).

That is easy to show using two stock cubes and some warm water. If one stock cube is placed in the bottom of one container, a crumbled stock cube is placed in the bottom of a second container, and an equal amount of warm water is added to each, the crumbled cube will dissolve faster.

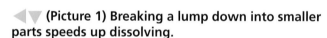 (Picture 1) Breaking a lump down into smaller parts speeds up dissolving.

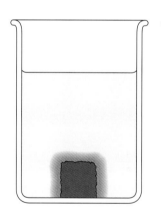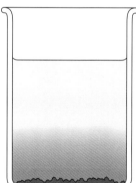

Why this happens

When something dissolves, the particles of the solid are pulled away by forces in the water. The crumbled stock cube dissolves much faster because the small pieces have a much bigger area in contact with the water than the larger cube. There are hundreds or thousands of surfaces in a crumbled cube. The large cube dissolves more slowly because the water can only get to the six sides of the cube—most of the cube remains out of reach of the water.

Stirring

Stirring can be as important as crumbling a lump into small pieces (Picture 2). To check this, add several spoonfuls of brown sugar to cold water in a glass. Add the same amount of sugar to an equal amount of cold water in a second glass.

The sugar will begin to dissolve slowly. By stirring the sugar in one of the glasses, you can make the sugar in that glass dissolve more quickly.

▶ (Picture 2) Stirring speeds up dissolving.

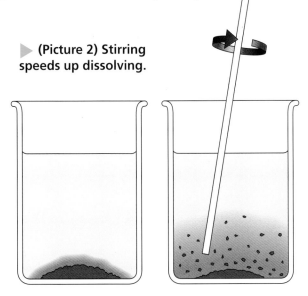

Why this happens

In the undisturbed glass the water next to the sugar soon takes up all the sugar it can and keeps sugar-free water from getting to the sugar. By stirring the water, the sugar-rich water is carried away, and sugar-free water is continually swept past the sugar grains.

Temperature

You may have noticed how useful hot water is in getting some substances to dissolve. In general, the hotter the solution, the faster a substance will dissolve in it *and* the more can be dissolved (Picture 3).

If you have two equal-sized containers, it is easy to show this difference. Pour hot water into one container and an equal amount of cold water into the second. Try to keep the hot water container warm, or do the experiment quickly before the water cools down. Now add a large spoonful of brown sugar to each container. You will find that the hot water dissolves the sugar far quicker than the cold water.

Summary

- **A powder will dissolve faster than a lump.**
- **Substances dissolve faster when they are stirred.**
- **Substances dissolve better when they are warmed.**

 SAFETY Never go near boiling water. Always get an adult to help.

▼ (Picture 3) Heat speeds up dissolving.

Why this happens

Hot water has more energy in it than cold water, and so the hot water pulls the sugar apart faster.

Dissolving adds volume

When one substance dissolves in another, it does not disappear, so it must take up space.

When one substance dissolves in another, it seems to disappear. But if you taste water that has salt dissolved in it, it still tastes salty, so you know that the salt is simply mixed up with the water. This means that salty water contains both water and salt. It must take up more space than the water alone.

Model dissolving by using beads

Dissolving can be hard to imagine, so it can be easier to see what is going on by using glass beads of different colors.

If you add a pile of red beads to a pile of green beads, the final pile will be bigger than either starting pile. In fact, it will be the same size as the two starting piles added together (Picture 1).

This is exactly the same when something dissolves. The only difference is that the "beads" are too small to see. For example, if you dissolve sugar in water, the grains of sugar are mixed up with the water, and they take up just as much space as they did before you dissolved them.

Sugar cube test

You can prove this by adding sugar cubes to water one at a time (Picture 2).

Begin with a clear jar, and pour 25ml of water into it. Mark the level of water on the jar with a felt-tip pen.

50 red beads   50 green beads

Volume 1   Volume 2

50 red beads and
50 green beads

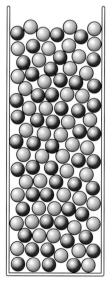

Volume of mixture = volume 1 + volume 2

▲ (Picture 1) When you mix grains of two substances together, the grains usually take up the same volume as the two substances did before they were mixed.

(Picture 2) A lot of sugar can be dissolved in water.

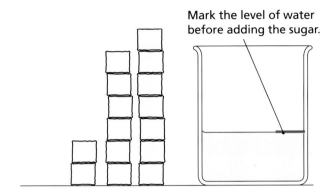

Mark the level of water before adding the sugar.

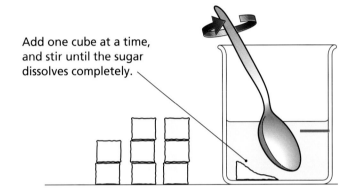

Add one cube at a time, and stir until the sugar dissolves completely.

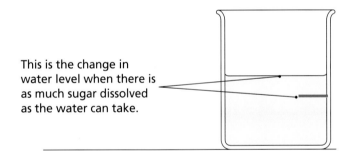

This is the change in water level when there is as much sugar dissolved as the water can take.

Add sugar cubes one at a time, and stir the solution after each addition.

When you have added the cubes, mark the level of water in the jar. If the sugar really did disappear, the water level would not change. On the other hand, if the sugar simply breaks down into tiny pieces that can no longer be seen, it will still be there, and so you will see the level of the solution rise.

(Picture 3) Relatively little salt can be dissolved in water.

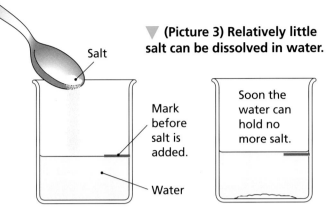

Salt

Mark before salt is added.

Water

Soon the water can hold no more salt.

In a glass jar containing 25ml of water you might be able to add about 15 sugar cubes (depending on the type and size of the cubes) before no more will dissolve. When no more sugar cubes will dissolve, stop adding.

In fact, after about 15 cubes have been added, the level of sugar water is much higher than before the sugar was added. This shows that dissolving a solid in a liquid causes the total volume to increase.

Other volume changes

The same experiment can be repeated with table salt or any other substance that dissolves, but a lot of sugar will dissolve in water (we say that sugar is very soluble), and so the change is easy to see. If you used salt, you would only get a slight increase in volume before you had dissolved as much salt as the water could hold (Picture 3).

Summary
- When a solid dissolves, the solution takes up more space.
- The amount of space taken up depends on how much of the solid dissolves.

Dissolving gases

Gases dissolve in liquids. A hot liquid can hold much less gas than a cold one, and liquids under pressure hold much more gas.

Gases can be dissolved in liquids naturally, for example, in the lava that comes from a volcano (Picture 1) or at the surface of the ocean, a lake, or a river. That is how oxygen gets into water so that fish and other water-living animals can breathe.

Where would you go in your home or school to find gas dissolved in water? The answer is only as far as the nearest tap, because all water contains dissolved air.

Getting the air out of water

Cold water can hold more air than hot water, so one way to see that water contains dissolved air is to heat it.

If you warm water, a few bubbles of air may be driven out (Picture 2). That is because you need to put a lot of energy into the water to drive the gas out. If

◀ (Picture 1) When lava rises up a volcano, there is less pressure on the gases dissolved in it. Gases form very quickly, exploding the lava into fragments called ash.

◀▼ (Picture 2) Leave a capped bottle of cold water to warm up, and water bubbles will begin to form.

Once cooled in the fridge, the airtight cap is screwed on to the bottle of water.

When taken out of the fridge and warmed, bubbles of gas are released.

you let water boil for a long time, you can drive out most of the air. (However, when you boil water, you also cause the water to turn into a gas—water vapor, or steam—so then the bubbles you see contain mostly steam.)

Getting the fizz into a drink

If you take the cap off a bottle of fizzy drink, the liquid immediately fills with bubbles that burst out at the surface (Picture 3).

The bubbles are made of a gas called carbon dioxide (the same gas that we breathe out from our lungs).

Very little carbon dioxide dissolves in fizzy drinks at room temperature. But under pressure enormous amounts of gas can be made to dissolve in the drink.

To add the fizz to soda or cola, it is first cooled so that it will soak up more gas. Then the liquid is placed in a chamber, with gas, under pressure. The liquid is then quickly bottled.

When the bottle is opened, the liquid is no longer under pressure, and it cannot hold as much gas. That is why the gas bursts out and makes the fizz.

Diver's "bends"

Although the amount of air that will dissolve in a liquid is normally quite small, the more pressure the liquid is put under, the more gas it can hold.

If you were to dive deep into the ocean, you would feel the pressure of

▶ (Picture 3) The stages of gas release when a fizzy drink cap is unscrewed slowly.

water on your body very quickly. When scuba divers go down, the deeper they go, the more of the air they are breathing dissolves in their blood. If the diver comes back to the surface quickly, the pressure goes down quickly, and the air comes back out of the blood and forms bubbles just as in a fizzy drink bottle. This condition is known as "the bends." It is extremely painful and may cause death. That is why divers have to return to the surface slowly enough for the air to come out of their blood without forming large bubbles.

Summary

- Gases dissolve in liquids.
- Gases are less soluble in hot liquids.
- Gases dissolve more easily under pressure.

Separating dissolved substances

Colored liquids may be made of many substances. You can sometimes find out what they are by using a filter paper.

A colored liquid, such as felt-tip pen ink, may look like a single color but is really a mixture of solids dissolved in water (Picture 1).

It is very hard to separate the various substances because they are dissolved in the water. However, you can see what they are made of if you get the colored ink to seep up a **POROUS** substance, like a filter paper (the kind used to filter coffee), because some colors will seep up the paper faster than others.

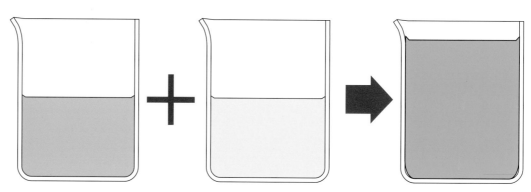

(Picture 1) A jar of blue paint added to a jar of yellow paint will produce a jar of green paint.

Measuring water dyes

Take several different water-based ink pens or dyes, and draw lines on the lower part of a filter cone. Now add clean water to the saucer it is sitting in. As the water rises up the filter paper, the different chemicals that make up the ink or dye are drawn up the paper at different speeds, as you can see in Picture 2.

As you watch the water creep up the paper, you will see that the original color first becomes blurred. This is the start of

the separation. The colors then begin to separate more clearly.

Could you guess which colors were needed to make up each ink or dye color?

The colors used to make inks and dyes may remind you of the colors of the rainbow, since most inks and dyes are made of mixtures of red, blue, and yellow.

Notice that an important property of the filter paper is that it lets liquid move up its surface. You could try other substances, such as newspaper, to see if they work as well.

Summary
- Most inks are mixtures of solids dissolved in liquid.
- Mixtures can be separated by drawing them up filter papers.

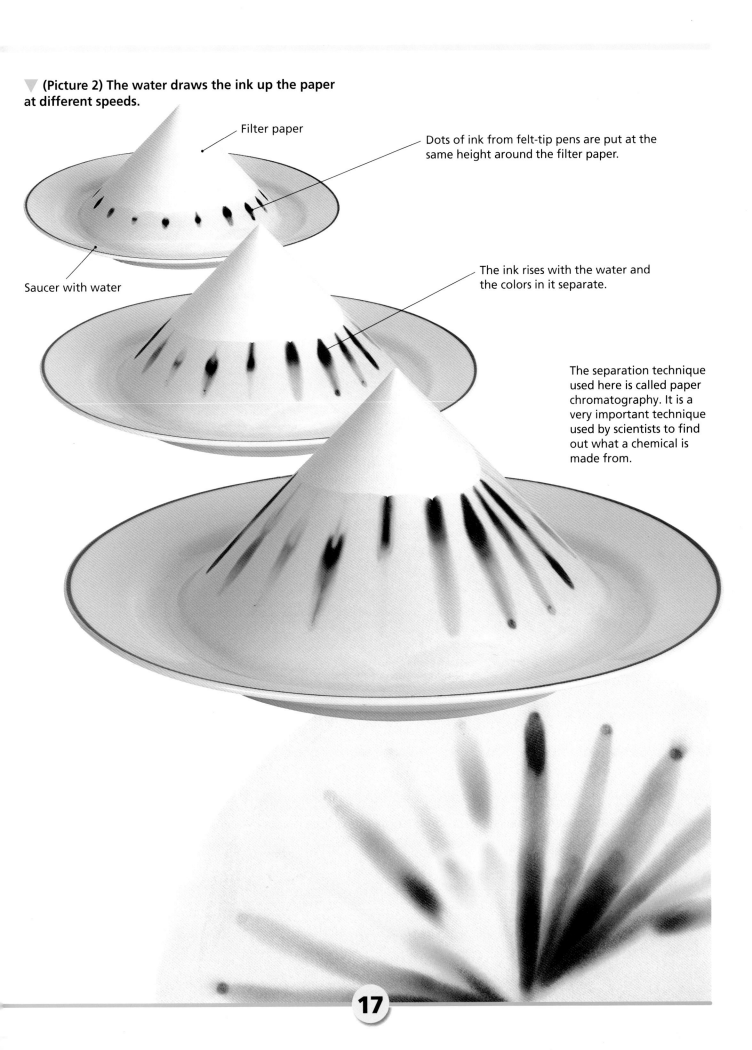

▼ **(Picture 2) The water draws the ink up the paper at different speeds.**

Filter paper

Dots of ink from felt-tip pens are put at the same height around the filter paper.

Saucer with water

The ink rises with the water and the colors in it separate.

The separation technique used here is called paper chromatography. It is a very important technique used by scientists to find out what a chemical is made from.

Crystals from solutions

You can grow CRYSTALS from solutions. Growing crystals is one way to separate solids from a solution.

In dissolving, a solid seems to disappear into a liquid. But, as we have seen, the solid is still there, only its particles are too small to see. Under special conditions it is possible to get the solid to come out of the solution again and at the same time grow into the most beautifully shaped crystals (Pictures 1 and 2).

Start with a concentrated solution

When you put sugar or salt into water, it dissolves. So how can you get a crystal to grow instead of dissolving? The answer is to begin with a solution that is so **CONCENTRATED** that no more solid will dissolve in it. To remind yourself about how this is done, see pages 8 and 9.

Choose a seed crystal

Once you have a really concentrated solution, you can begin to grow a crystal. Start off with a small crystal of the same substance that you made the solution from. For example, if you have made up a salt solution, then you need to use a small salt crystal, such as a grain of rock salt—they are bigger and easier to handle than grains of table salt. If you are using a sugar solution, then you can

▲▼ (Pictures 1 and 2) The blue crystal above was grown from a tiny seed crystal. The longer the crystals remain in the solution, the larger they will grow—the one below took two weeks to grow.

use a sugar grain, a sugar cube, or even a piece of sugary hard candy. It will be your seed crystal.

If a crystal is to grow evenly all around, it must be held up in the solution. If you simply put it at the bottom of the jar with the solution, it can only grow upward, and it will have a flat base.

To suspend a crystal, tie a piece of fine cotton thread around the seed crystal, and tie the other end around a stick or pencil that will fit across the top of the container (Pictures 3 and 4).

Cover the top of the container. You don't want the solution to **EVAPORATE** (turn into gas) while the crystals are growing, or the crystals will be very small.

Now the only thing you need to do is wait. It may take days, or even weeks, for large crystals to form. They will form only if the solution is left completely undisturbed.

▼ **(Pictures 3 and 4) Growing large crystals in a concentrated sugar solution.**

Summary

- **Growing crystals is one way of separating solids from a solution.**
- **Crystals will only grow in saturated solutions— solutions in which no more of a substance will dissolve.**
- **Crystals grow slowly.**

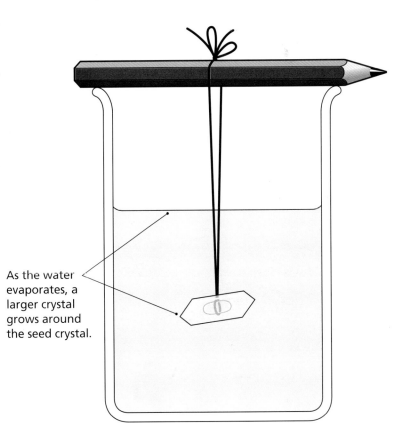

Thread used to hold the seed crystal. The thread is tied to a pencil or stick to hold it in place.

The solution contains as much sugar as it can hold.

A very small piece of sugary candy is used as a seed crystal.

As the water evaporates, a larger crystal grows around the seed crystal.

Recovering dissolved substances

When water is allowed to EVAPORATE, or if it is boiled off, the solid substances that were dissolved in it are left behind.

As you have seen, a solution contains a mixture of substances dissolved in a liquid. You can't get the dissolved substances out of the liquid by filtering, so how do you separate them? The answer is by taking away the liquid.

There are two ways that a liquid, such as water, can be separated from the substances dissolved in it. They are called evaporating and **BOILING**. They both work by changing the water to steam (which is a gas). In each case anything dissolved in the water will be left behind after all the water has changed to gas.

Evaporating

If you leave a saltwater solution for several hours or days, the water will slowly evaporate, but the salt that was dissolved in it will not. Instead, the salt will be left behind (Picture 1).

Evaporation will speed up if the air above the water is dry. One way to keep dry air above the water is to blow air over it or put the dish of water in a breeze.

Another way of speeding up evaporation is to warm the air. Yet another way is to warm the water. The more warmth there is, the more **ENERGY** there is to make the water change from a liquid to a gas.

▼ **(Picture 1) The stages of evaporation.**

1. A glass bowl containing water. Salt is added, and the solution is stirred until no more salt will dissolve.

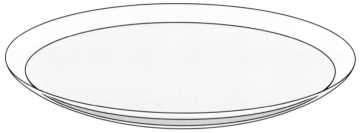

2. Over time, evaporation removes water, and the water level goes down. A thin film of salt appears on the edge of the bowl.

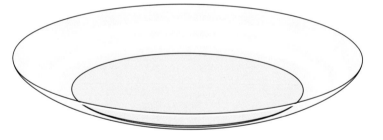

2. Evaporation is complete. Only the dissolved solids remain.

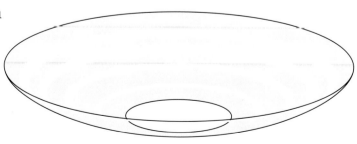

Much of the sea salt we use is made by letting seawater evaporate in lagoons that are heated by the Sun (Pictures 2 and 3).

Boiling

Boiling is a fast form of evaporation. By boiling the water, you are putting a large amount of heat energy into the water and making the water change from liquid to gas as fast as possible.

Boiling is sometimes used for getting the salt out of seawater so that it is fit to drink and free from impurities. In this case the boiling produces steam, and the steam is cooled before it can mix with the rest of the air. When the steam is cooled, the water changes back into a liquid. This is called **CONDENSATION**. Once the condensed water has been collected and cooled, it is ready for drinking (Picture 4).

▲▶ **(Pictures 2 and 3)** The sea contains huge amounts of salt. People collect this sea salt by allowing the seawater to evaporate in lagoons. They are called salt pans. Because water evaporates faster when the water and the air are warm, most salt pans are found in places with warm climates, not cold ones.

Summary

- Dissolved substances can be separated from water by removing the water.
- Evaporation is a slow way to remove water.
- Boiling is a fast way to remove water.

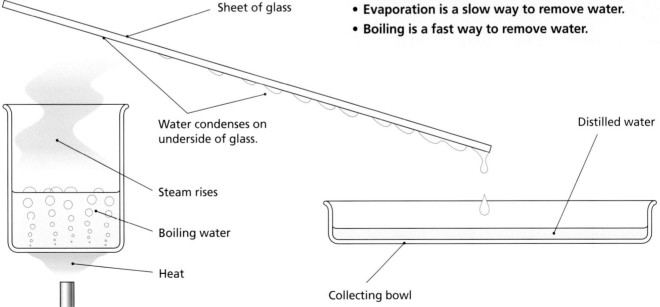

Sheet of glass

Water condenses on underside of glass.

Steam rises

Boiling water

Heat

Distilled water

Collecting bowl

▲ **(Picture 4) The principle of how condensation is used to make pure water by boiling. Pure water made from boiling is called distilled water.**

SAFETY Never go near boiling water. Always get an adult to help.

Dissolving rocks

Limestone rock dissolves in rainwater. It causes spectacular caves, hard water, and "furred-up" teapots.

Limestone and chalk rock are natural substances that dissolve in rainwater. Over millions of years water dissolves the rock, and that causes caves to form. However, the limestone is easily made to come out of the water; and when this happens, it makes rock again (Picture 1).

Hard water

When limestone is dissolved in streams and tap water, the water is called **HARD WATER**.

You can easily tell if you have hard tap water. Go to a tap, and try making a lather with soap and water (Picture 2). If your hands stay scummy and you can't get much of a lather, you live in an area with limestone dissolved in the water.

▲ (Picture 1) The needlelike columns that hang from the roofs (stalactites) or grow from the floors (stalagmites) of caves are places where water containing dissolved limestone drips from the roof of the cave and splashes on the floor. When the water evaporates, the limestone remains. In both places the limestone has come out of solution and formed rock.

"Fur" in teapots

Another way to check for hard water is to look inside a teapot. If you see a white coating on the inside—called "fur" (Picture 3)—you have a coating of limestone rock inside your teapot!

Getting the limestone out of water

Limestone dissolves in cold water. But limestone is, unusually, less soluble in hot water. So when the limestone is heated,

▲ (Picture 2) Hard water will not form lather with soap but makes a scum instead.

it comes out of solution. That is why the inside of a teapot "furs" up.

Boiling some eggs in cold water in a clean, nonstick (Teflon or glass) saucepan (Picture 4) shows how the limestone in eggshells comes out of solution as it heats up. Once the eggs have boiled for a while, take them out, and pour the water away safely. Let the pan cool, then look inside. The limestone makes a white film on the surface.

It is possible to remove dissolved limestone from water. The device that does this is called a water softener. Some people in hard water areas have water softeners installed in their homes.

Summary

- **Hard water contains dissolved limestone.**
- **Heating makes limestone come out of solution.**
- **Limestone will cause "fur" on teapots.**

⚠ **SAFETY** Never go near boiling water. Always get an adult to help.

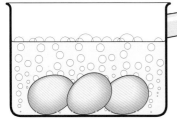

▲ (Picture 4) Boil some eggs in water in a nonstick pan for several minutes (as though you were hard-boiling the eggs), and then pour the water away. Let it cool down completely, and you will be able to see a white limestone film on the nonstick surface. It will wipe off onto your finger.

▼ (Picture 3) The "fur" on a heating element is limestone that has come out of solution and made rock.

Index

Science Matters!

Grolier Educational

First published in the United States in 2003 by Grolier Educational, Sherman Turnpike, Danbury, CT 06816

Copyright © 2003
Atlantic Europe Publishing Company Ltd.

Author
Brian Knapp, BSc, PhD

Educational Consultant
Peter Riley, BSc, C Biol, MI Biol, PGCE

Art Director
Duncan McCrae, BSc

Senior Designer
Adele Humphries, BA, PGCE

Editor
Lisa Magloff, BA

Illustrations
David Woodroffe

Designed and produced by
Earthscape Editions

Reproduced in Malaysia by
Global Color

Printed in Hong Kong by
Wing King Tong Company Ltd

Picture credits
All photographs are from the Earthscape Editions photolibrary.

Library of Congress Cataloging-in-Publication Data

Knapp, Dr. Brian J.
  Science Matters! / [Dr. Brian J. Knapp].
    p. cm.
  Includes index.
  Summary: Presents information on a wide variety of topics in basic biology, chemistry, and physics.
  Contents: v. 1. Food, teeth, and eating—v. 2. Helping plants grow well—v. 3. Properties of materials—v. 4. Rocks and soils—v. 5. Springs and magnets—v. 6. Light and shadows—v. 7. Moving and growing—v. 8. Habitats—v. 9. Keeping warm and cool—v. 10. Solids and liquids—v. 11. Friction—v. 12. Simple electricity—v. 13. Keeping healthy—v. 14. Life cycles—v. 15. Gases around us—v. 16. Changing from solids to liquids to gases—v. 17. Earth and beyond—v. 18. Changing sounds—v. 19. Adapting and surviving—v. 20. Microbes—v. 21. Dissolving—v. 22. Changing materials—v. 23. Forces in action—v. 24. How we see things—v. 25. Changing circuits.
  ISBN 0-7172-5834-3 (set)—ISBN 0-7172-5835-1 (v. 1)—ISBN 0-7172-5836-X (v. 2)—ISBN 0-7172-5837-8 (v. 3)—ISBN 0-7172-5838-6 (v 4)—ISBN 0-7172-5839-4 (v. 5)—ISBN 0-7172-5840-8 (v. 6)—ISBN 0-7172-5841-6 (v. 7)—ISBN 0-7172-5842-4 (v. 8)—ISBN 0-7172-5843-2 (v. 9)—ISBN 0-7172-5844-0 (v. 10)—ISBN 0-7172-5845-9 (v. 11)—ISBN 0-7172-5846-7 (v. 12)—ISBN 0-7172-5847-5 (v. 13)—ISBN 0-7172-5848-3 (v. 14)—ISBN 0-7172-5849-1 (v. 15)—ISBN 0-7172-5850-5 (v. 16)—ISBN 0-7172-5851-3 (v. 17)—ISBN 0-7172-5852-1 (v. 18)—ISBN 0-7172-5853-X (v. 19)—ISBN 0-7172-5854-8 (v. 20)—ISBN 0-7172-5855-6 (v. 21)—ISBN 0-7172-5856-4 (v. 22)—ISBN 0-7172-5857-2 (v. 23)—ISBN 0-7172-5858-0 (v. 24)—ISBN 0-7172-5859-9 (v. 25)
  1. Science—Juvenile literature. [1. Science.] I. Title.

Q163.K48 2002
500—dc21
                                                    2002017302